"With intensely imaginative verse, *Voices of Iona* entreats the soul of the sojourner to meditate upon the subtle signals of transcendence that penetrate the shadows of our human condition. Themes of historical rootedness, finding the sacred in the everyday present, and the universal longing for our true home inspire deep reflection upon one's own pilgrimage. This collection is a rare treasure."

—Melissa Cain Travis, president, Society for Women of Letters

"I'm so grateful for this contemplative pilgrimage towards transformation, awareness of our place in God's world, and the power of prayerful introspection. Through these poems, Fullman takes the reader on a series of journeys away from the chaotic present into places where 'time and history continually fold back upon themselves as we follow the steps of others' towards the pilgrim's ultimate destination: our divine home."

—Scott Manor, president, Knox Theological Seminary

"Fullman leads his readers on a pilgrimage from the Cliffs of Dover to the monastery founded by St. Columba on the Scottish isle of Iona. His verse carries us on with rhythms that are incantatory yet colloquial, subtle yet resonant. This long poem enacts a dialogue between ancient Celtic myths and modern voices. It is at once profoundly learned and deeply personal."

—Ben Lockard, former president, T. S. Eliot Society

Voices of Iona

Voices of Iona

Joshua S. Fullman

RESOURCE *Publications* · Eugene, Oregon

VOICES OF IONA

Resource Publications
An Imprint of Wipf and Stock Publishers
199 W. 8th Ave., Suite 3
Eugene, OR 97401

www.wipfandstock.com

PAPERBACK ISBN: 978-1-6667-5523-7
HARDCOVER ISBN: 978-1-6667-5524-4
EBOOK ISBN: 978-1-6667-5525-1

11/02/22

Contents

Foreword

AS THE FIFTH CENTURY opened, the Roman Empire was in a state of hazardous decline. It had survived a tumultuous plague, the relocation of its bureaucratic center to the east, a series of devastating Germanic invasions, the division of its behemoth kingdom into territories, and a seismic shift in religious culture. The peace that for centuries had been purchased on the frontiers of war had finally broken, and those wars were brought increasingly close to home. None since Sulla and then Julius Caesar had been thought a credible threat to international security; and while the edges might be fraying, the center was still holding. Many could still console themselves with the glory that was once, even if the reality was less than inspiring now. But in 410, the unthinkable occurred. Rome, the Eternal City which had stood for nearly a thousand years, was destroyed by the Goths. In desperation, legions were recalled from the far reaches of the empire, including from the western outpost of Britannia; but the effort was too little and too late. Rome would become the last victim of its own imperial machine, and as St. Jerome said, "The city which had taken the whole world was itself taken."

We can imagine the chaos that would have gripped millions of anxious Roman citizens. Rome had been, so they thought, the light in the cultural darkness, a bulwark against barbarism that had unexpectedly crumbled. Countless souls, now displaced and afraid, no doubt racked their minds wondering, "Where did we go wrong?" and "How could this have happened?" and "What do we do now?" These questions have been repeated by all peoples in the wake of cataclysms like the Black Death, the Lisbon earthquake, or in the tumult of global war and the impending threat of nuclear annihilation. Indeed, to the Romans at that time, it must have seemed like the end of the world—and though the western half of the Empire would struggle onward for another sixty-five years, it certainly would have seemed the end of their world.

In his magnum opus, *City of God*, St. Augustine of Hippo looked out over the gray skies of an apocalyptic landscape and caught a fiery ray of hope. While Christians and pagans alike lamented the loss of their way of life, he heard the promise of the future. The fall of Rome revealed that, no matter the strength of our desires, we can never sufficiently understand the world, nor make it safe enough to withstand the chaos. Here, then, was a chance for renewal. Here God and man could write the next phase of human history. Life might indeed become harder without the protection of the legions and the institutional stability of the senate, but perhaps that was a blessing incognito. For our lives are not anchored in the fixtures of civilization but in the ethereal world beyond. Those fixtures are only symbols, signposts on the road toward the Heavenly Jerusalem. We are not residents of Rome, he insisted, but pilgrims looking for home.

His prophetic words were confidently prescient. Post-Roman Europe became shaky ground for a Christendom appearing to fragment and decentralize. But what many assumed was the end turned out to be only a beginning, as the story of Christ spread throughout the continent. Certain mission fields took root and became specialized places for education, for hospitals, for art and agriculture, for community. The hermetical retreats of Syria and Egypt where penitents clothed themselves in the white martyrdom of the desert were reproduced and codified in the rigor of monastic order and in the retreat of pilgrimage. Mount Sinai, Monte Cassino, Cluny, Kildaire. All of these and more provided waystations for believers to fortify their faith in sacred places, to practice homelessness, to find physical and spiritual healing, to right their souls, and to prepare for the End—and for their end. Pilgrimage became, for many medieval Christians, the reenactment of the Augustinian ideal. For centuries to come, a great number of shrines and holy places began to spring up all over Europe. Canterbury, St. James of Compostela, Palestine.

Back in Britannia, off the west coast of what was then called Dál Riata, on the edge of the former empire, still rests a lonely isle. In the crosswaters of Scotland, Ireland, and England, it is central enough to be reached by merchants and raiders but far enough away from the concerns of the mainland—from a world just as busy, just as harried, just as confused and uncertain of its future as our own. Iona was founded as a monastery by St. Columba over a hundred years after Augustine's pronouncement, and it became a sacred locus for pilgrims to find themselves and to meet with God. The modern traveler can see that it is an unideal location to start a church, but it is a perfect place to raise a shrine. Pilgrimage should bring about reflection, meditation, contemplation, illumination; Iona would offer all this and more—a place, as Chaucer's *Parson's Tale* reminds us, for transformation. A great cloud of witnesses, all those who came before, from St. Columba to George Macleod, would gather here to spur the pilgrim on to charity and to good works. Heaven and earth would meet on this humble island, and the invisible Kingdom perhaps never felt more tangible than in Iona's magnificent rocks, its beige sands, and its paradisal, clear blue waters that stretch into an azure horizon.

*

In 2008, I went on pilgrimage. Not in the medieval sense; in fact, I didn't even know it was pilgrimage at the time. I thought I was packing up my family from our comfortable lives in the States to study at the University of Edinburgh as another step on what I hoped would be a promising academic career. And so I did. But my removal from home, from the familiar cultural touchstones of fast food, high-speed internet, a congested network of superhighways, the clash of steel and neon, and ubiquitous advertising in every stretch and turn of the eyes remade me. From our staging place in the Scottish capital, we drove its lowlands, walked its highlands, discovered its islands, crafting a pilgrim road that would eventually lead us around the globe.

To say all was easy and exciting would be grossly untrue, as anyone who has had to radically change their palate knows. All anchors of knowledge—cultural, moral, aesthetic—were unmoored. A stranger in a strange land, I was forced, in very painful ways at first but later in a liturgical, gradual unwinding of the mind, to become something more. Prayer was no longer a daily fireside chat but an urgent need to outpour my soul and encounter a living presence. I experienced both the embrace of community and the terrifying but necessary isolation of self-knowledge. I learned to accomplish simple acts of faith, trained my eyes with the vision to hope, found meditation in the stillness and peace in the conflict. In truth, I relearned how to live.

Pilgrimage, the stripping away of all artifice to discover the soul within, compels us to recall forgotten truths: that man's life does not consist in the abundance of his possessions, that what passes for fruitful labor is often self-marketing career promotion, that the preservation of one's image aborts the agonizing work of self-denial, that the offering of forgiveness and charity embodies Love in all its fulness. Pilgrimage gently thrusts us out of the weight of our own inertia and pushes us to live in the Kingdom where heaven and earth truly meet.

We have forgotten this essential spiritual discipline. In the wake of the Protestant Reformation and the discovery of the Americas, the theme of pilgrimage was, we may say, replaced by the myth of the new world and by idealized visions of a more perfect state. Perhaps as a consequence, with our eyes to the horizon, we do not know how to live in the present. Our minds drift too easily into the stream of years gone by, where we fret about our mistakes or relive curated images of a perfect past. Or worries about the future press themselves too urgently upon us, robbing us of rumination and contentment. Harried as we are, the twenty-first century does not hold over other ages a monopoly on busyness, overextension, and exhaustion. Other ages have born their share of burdens as well, with more fear of danger than we often suffer. They, too, needed retreat and recuperation. But today's typical vacation prompts distraction, not reflection—and we often return more ragged and disappointed than when we began. The iconoclasm of modernity assumes a break between language and experience, and so we believe, much to our loss, the pilgrim road is merely a meaningful jaunt, a way to stretch our legs and see new sights but nothing more. And even for those who would wish to walk it, not many will afford the expense or peril.

However, if we cannot make the journey to Croagh Patrick or to Canterbury Cathedral, we can still encounter the sacred spaces of life in glimpses of that other world. This revelation is no surprise to many, especially those who find the time to reflect in the wilds of nature, the cultivation of a garden, or in the colors and textures of art. Poetry, to those who have ears to hear, can transport us there. Its minute attention to detail, its balance of sound and sense furrows the dry, baked soil of the mind, unearthing new rows to receive old truths. In verse the imagination grasps something ephemeral, even something eternal. An apt word, a resonant line, even a whole stanza can transport us elsewhere, to understand the enigma—or merely to marvel at it—and say to ourselves, *Yes, of course, it has always been thus. Why hadn't I seen it before?*

The poems in this collection long for the culmination of time, the reverberation of a golden age fingered in the present with eyes ahead to the future. For in pilgrimage, time and history continually fold back upon themselves as we follow the steps of others, repeating a cycle that will come to fruition in us and in those who come after. Each experience in these pieces is unique: some of them real and some mystical (though perhaps not less real); some are true and some fictional (though, too, perhaps not less true); and all of them are shared by someone who passed that way before. If the saying is accurate that we take something of a place with us when we leave, and we also leave part of ourselves behind in that place, then historical memory must be a fathomless well indeed. And the touch of Stonehenge's monoliths, the Gothic towers of Notre Dame, the imbibing of the Sacrament, or the sounds of Iona's shores all echo with the orchestra of fellow pilgrims past and future.

St. Augustine closes his treatise looking forward to the felicity enjoyed in the Heavenly City. As fallen people, we begin as citizens of Babylon, of London, of New York and Los Angeles— all of them erections of temporary security built east of Eden. But our broken psyche longs to return home, and the human condition can be summarized in endless attempts to regain wholeness and immortality. The construction of cities, utopian political hopes, the formation of legacies—and even, perhaps especially, art itself—depicts the low, agonized groans of creation. The divine pilgrimage from Babylon to Jerusalem is an arduous road made of clay that, as we walk, transforms into golden glass. And each day we consciously choose to walk the pilgrim road, whether on foot or in the metrical feet of poetry, we hear ever more clearly the familiar and welcoming sounds of home.

Montgomery, Alabama
August 31, 2022

Acknowledgements

MOST PEOPLE IMAGINE A poet sitting on the shore with a notebook or at the typewriter sipping wine when the Muse calls. Those are some pleasant moments, to be sure, but rare among the more common moments of grinding frustration trying to reconstruct a stanza or proofread a manuscript for the typesetter or brainstorm marketing strategies. In short, poetry is creative release wrapped in art and packaged in business. Which means there are many players involved in the production.

I want to thank several by name who have played their various roles. First, as always, is my wife, the Lady Fullman, who defends my work tooth and nail with all of her savvy, and who, more importantly, shared the pilgrim road with me. I would also like to thank Andrew Jacobs, who received the first draft of the manuscript and went through the painstaking task of responding to each piece. Allen Mendenhall and Layne Keele advised me in the challenges of publication and legal maneuverings of contracts, respectively, for which I am in their debt. Finally, I would also like to thank the staff at Wipf & Stock for their solid feedback and assistance in the publication process. To each of you, I give my humble gratitude.

Several of these poems were first published in various journals before making their appearance here. For the editors of those journals who thought them worthy of publication, I am thankful.

- "Harvest Poem," *The Wordsmith Journal Magazine*, September 2013

- "Everything," *Images in Ink*, Fall 2019

- "Trans Migration," *W-Poesis*, April 2021

- "Snow at Morning," *W-Poesis*, April 2021

ACKNOWLEDGEMENTS

- "Emhain Ablach," *The Mythic Circle* 43, 2021
- "A Midwinter's Song," *The North American Anglican Review*, April 2022

Centuries on Dover

I.

The cliffs are our first effects,
the first resurgence from the deep,
forever luminous,

mute sentinels of an iron island
kingdom of crumbling stones and sand,
shining transfigured in the mind,

fractals of rememory where days
once lived, though not by us,
stroll the banks again in holy contemplation.

Not a taste, you see, not a word
that lingers on the tongue like claret,
but a whisper on water

so piercing we strain to hear,
a bone chill in the air soaked by eons
of dreamers wishing they could live here

in the long ago.

II.

Yet beneath the plumb of sight,
these same cold waters thought receding
birthed white towers in their might

where time in millions measures.
Its thick pulse thrumbs and feeds
the vain leviathan we flee

while luring him on shore. Their blades
assault the spectral beach and thrones
of ivory, still undeterred

to claw down that imagined world
we love. But no melancholy beast
nor futile Gallish curse

can bow these cliffs. They also
are part of earth and man and time,
for change is the great tide

of the living.

    III.

The sea's hands break upon the world
with desperate cries of peace—
and then in fury sound retreat

before charging once again.
A courageous hour lulls
in cowardly expectation.

Here the Christ Druid sidles
through the fog. I see him,
somehow, shadowing every mist.

The Hebrew stone and Celtic sky
he wanders, contemplating
a Socratic catechism in a shard of glass.

And I, listening to the waves,
cannot hear him speak—only the sad,
eternal note—but stand

unbowed.

IV.

We cross the shore, sojourned Vikings,
imagining some conquest,
passing in and out of time,

aware these cliffs will long survive
barbaric claims—these who witnessed,
you remind me, the conqueror's greed,

the king's bondage, and the poet's farewell,
watch us mount the hill, bear secret pictures
of a home already fading

as old world swallows new. The landscape
steals back, with casual reciprocity,
our deaf, naïve demands to find

in her ourselves. We hover, still,
above the glacial calm, unaware
the dance of sea and land will soon

become our own.

Culture Shock

It passes your lips, furtively
at first, after the waitress turns
away, her punk pink hair a buoy

bobbing backward. Glazing the fare
before, rejecting toads in holes,
scorched eggs, and Welsh rabbits, you flopped

on eggs partnered with tomatoes,
the path of least resistance, sure
that Yorkshire substance shares no kin

with Jello. But no travel books
devoured during the flight, your course
in Burns and Boswell, nor the tastes

of traveling websites mention this
strange, blackened cake. No matter. You
dwell cleft, a disembodied shell,

a ten-hour abstraction across
a pond, uncertain of the time,
unwilling to ignore the gall

of an angry paunch. Then the smell
of sausage, texture faint with oats,
and its sharp metallic taste strikes

you sober and wakes your senses;
even somnolent you can't forget
your first.

Weeks pass, at market there

you see the now familiar dish
and ask its name. The chequer smiles,
invites you in the outside joke—

and though your bile rises at the thought,
laughing timid with her, you long
to slip again into the taste

of blood pudding.

The Wall (I.)

The bowed and docile grass, so long mowed down,
    thrusts upward round its neighbor rocks.
    Through centuries this earth and stone
and mortar stands above the layered shelves
    of dust named Vindolanda,

trumpeting to stolid tourists after all,
    there's something still prefers a wall,
    unaltered by the spit of time—
a poisoned frost in soil and soul, that none
    protect your lineage nor home.

An infinite and curious tranquil green
    stretch equal here from north to south—
    yet in this step the axe of Hadrian falls,
cleaves deep where sheep might graze or men despoil
    and rain still justly roil.

What global dreams were etched before this wall?
    What broke beneath its calloused curves?
    Would Roman stand for foreign dirt?
Would Celt transgress some bony, tyrant line
    to hail an idol bird?

Via Vaccarum

The mute shriek of two-thirty mocks
the sleepless dreamer—no time
for anything but in between these sheets.

But louder still the encroaching gawker
this wet, rainless night, crowds his angst
on my dull mind and, like the time, betrays me.

Barely there, I wonder if I hear his shouts
striking the cobbled streets—or is it history's echoes
of a thousand ancient voices wandering the drunken cowgate?

His screams, their screams, dormant in the day,
unmask secret terrors none dare sober contemplate.
He sees, I'd wager, familiar unnamed faces

trading cattle in another age, the bovine stench of flatulence
        and fear,
wearing their dread like heavy leather ambivalence
and knowing slaughter was the boulevard toward home.

Gone quiet now, awake. Did he
lose steam? make up with his old lady?
or did he plunge into the dank cobblestones

and scrape his skull on centuries of filth?
I turn over slowly—lest my movement rouse
his voice—just thankful not to hear the screams.

Birdwatching

When the foreigner, every act a mirror,
feeling yourself from outside
as others see you—every speech a stage
for another's carnival.

So I pop in at the pub,
smelling stares in stiletto eyes
adjudicating over steaming pork and leeks,
but fearing more the ones whose eyes don't rise.

And as the warm beer froths
around an icy hand, I taste the foam
of monks and ploughmen refusing to forget
centuries of Vikings, Frenchmen, and Mohammedons.

The street lamps sieged by fog
surround each glowing stroller at night
where white paneled vans point microphones
listening for insurgents and unlicensed tele signals,

and I move my cursor carefully in an internet café,
each hurry or delay an analytic plot,
read and re-read and think about my thoughts
that they already thought before me.

But then my professor invites her graduates home
for a pint and a pirate smile;
surely MI5 wouldn't send a butterfly
to light on American students of medieval literature. And yet.

Suddenly, I overhear a seditious campus
conversation, intrigued, only to realize
it was I who spoke the words. And I wonder,
what home will be left when I return?

and my eyes, wrenched open by a leprous orange torch glow grinning madly through the pane, bleed the last drops of moisture remaining. The emigrant sirens without and torpid thirst within nibble at my nerves, break my sleep, and thrust this fierce sojourn to the thin shroud of reality. A crumbling flat, though no monastic cell, befits a desert vestibule. How many days now? Daring to rise, I stumble through the grimy air and dig down under carpet into plied wood with long nails, and, still dreaming, search for pearls—but overturn stones just to discover rocks. He once asked what tempts me here—and, strange, I have nothing true to say but a half-hearted exile self-imposed. The regret of regret. Where winds the wind? Were there even sand dunes to save me from this waste—but not even a mirage slakes the angst. The meter, long broken, cannot catch the pouring thoughts from every sieve and strain—so I wander a world of brick roads, black with time and red with rain long-past, where memories of Egyptian ease turn me westward, where streets are named, and clothed in the same for more than one bloody block. I recall the California lounges of poisoned asps and the scourge of sloth. But here, might I make out just the willed whisper of a word, passing like a prophet's revelation through the humid, heavy scent? Yet for now, on the fringe of being, beyond candlelit dinners in the penthouses above, friendless to the bodies below, I sit among the rubbish waiting fire, a smith clutching iron—or a second flood, a wright with rib. Might I turn back? Aye, and lose it all; the crooked climb saves from the fall. Might I cling to the wind? I stand fast, lest luxury wither these hands. And far away, the thunder crawls forward

Trans Migration

A crack in the concrete
jars the stroller, spills my son,
catapults both our futures
into the cobblestone streets
as the swerving taxi
and apathetic city
rush by.

I scoop up his tears,
hold him violently
with fatherly impotence:
we won't always be pilgrims,
I whisper, not always missing keys
or lost coins.

Yet he screams despite,
recoiling from strange babel,
wishing the flat will just be warm,
that the sun will rise
for more than five cold hours.

I fear he'll retreat
into himself,
never rising from this valley,
island highlands passing.

So we grapple one another,
the city plunging past,
fire finding light in the dark.

And the pitch of our
mutual tumult crescendos into a

singularity.

The Wall (II.)

Here is the line Caesar—Hail!—fixed us. Here I must stand
    on my own strength.
Marching the streets of the fortress I list all the howls
    and the vile oaths
Heaped at the wall. In the dark lies the nothing beyond:
    only checked by
Radiant shines of the braziers that lade and impregn all
    the blank space.
Still, out there enemy fires brush the landscape, raise sweat
    from my creased brow,
Knowing their rebel flames die not. I listen to silences, will my
People to sleep tranquil, tighten the grip of my sword,
    standing sure, strong,
Ready to cast out the monsters that threat our serenity,
    break stones,
Snuff down the light. Thus, we honor the dead with our
    adamant last stand:
My fallen brother, who, shamelessly slain by marauders
    and their dark
Druid weeks past, was interred by the sexton. Two shillings
    and one pint
Cost me his passage to fortresses below—though some
    among us say
Good men await a return by the power of a great god's death.
So I salute him and pray power to tame this black, savage isle,
    lest the
Wild finally triumph in men's dim hearts, branches that grow
    an unripened
Fruit, proper only for burning—to spread the imperial light.

The Gododdin

I.

In Athens
the gods are shaped
by stone and fear
and speak
an unknown language.

But in the smoky north,
men are shriven
and broken
by the spirit's mist
and chant the iron.

II.

We who remained
sat, after, around
the table, drinking mead,
songs slowly rising
as the torrent poured outside.

And I, too, blood-drenched
for the sake of my song,
survived to find a desert
of festal memories.
What then did we save?

III.

The whispers
of names become
the breath of builders
shaping cities
from the ruins.

And what
warriors break
and gods destroy,
kings rebuild
with stiffer monuments.

IV.

Our children following
will erect Cardiff,
Glamis, Warwick,
cross the sea and forge
other, mightier works.

None in the New
World yet speak. But
the darkening clouds hang
ominous over another, denser
island of rising towers.

V.

In the waves
of death we stand,
sowing teeth in the mud
of yesterday's anxieties,
birthing tomorrow's wars.

But we drink tonight,
brothers, and shout our spirits
over the night fires
to a new age,
and an age never to come.

A Saturday Run

Prince's Street:
the sun rises over a dozen spires,
peaks, capitals, and cathedrals—
pikes piercing sky shout
their pride to the clouds

   When will the baby just sleep through the night?

Victoria Street:
bouncing on stone block sidewalks
like the queen's messenger
or a delinquent soldier reporting
for duty, inhaling the wind's refuse—
a thick layer of paper mill sulfur

   Will I pass my exams?—Wait, did I even pay the bursar
   for my exams yet?

South Bridge:
I hurtle past buildings of glass
and steel, homes of quarried king's
architecture, separated by
centuries and a quick jaunt. No time
to breathe with the merging of time

   When is the mouthy neighbor upstairs supposed
   to move out?

Lauriston Place:
where dentists sit in storefronts
recently rented by apothecaries

and printers two centuries ago,
never noticing each other

Will the redhead in the coffee shop be there this morning?

Middle Meadow Walk:
the park the city's self-restraint,
the medicine of nature.
The distant view of crags and peaks
reminding us the dead
still sing of dreams their own

*Will she like the sight of my legs? And what will she
be wearing?*

Melville Drive to Hope Park Terrace:
A famous restaurant, a chain,
reminds me of home,
pulling me backward to the future
like a suffocating flame

Can I make it?

St. Leonard Street:
dodging suddenly an unclaimed bag
of rubbish, I press into a pool
of vomit from someone's late night binge.

Sighing, I turn back, walk home,
filling with vain questions
and ignoring the squish of my shoes.

The Thistle and the Sickle

Drowning in the stacks of tomes
                 from shelves built long and tall
and centuries before her time,
                 she does not swim but stares
through stained glass walls
                 at rain-soaked skies, imagines
one day leaving university
                 to secure a civil sinecure
and hide indoors
                 from harsher storms than these.

Thick with phlem and rummaging
                 through piles and mounds and peaks
of post, he sorts the bills
                 from benefits and subdivides
the addresses whose routes
                 he'll trudge another fifteen years
to dress—one day—in just
                 his robe and breathlessly
unseal his own brown envelopes
                 and drink his pension cheque.

She stands beneath the stark
                 John Lewis sign, decked out
in a rack suit and gossiping
                 of one thrilling night of ecstasy
with some lover yet unnamed,
                 charming all her work mates
while they each turn away their eyes
                 from waving customers needing help

to find a fourteen stone dress
                          or a pair of matching pumps.

Fatigued by flickering fantasies
                          on screen, he shouts out grudgingly
along the hall for what-
                          ever patient next in line,
then needles them for symptoms,
                          confirming his diagnosis
before they clear their mouths,
                          inward hoping just to find
an epidemic—or at the least,
                          a fascinating case.

None notice Hume once studied
                          in these rooms, and Smith shared
coffee while Burns threw poetry.
                          Today the conversation dries
and once proud flowers wilt,
                          few of them ever realizing
their longing for Iona. Instead,
                          their stems retreat at pompous threats
and ever-empty dreams—
                          the dull blade of dependency.

Vox Populi

A common crown
A common throne
A common reign for all

A common life
A common death
A common cattle call

Underground
(*Mary King's Close*)

Below the mountains and metropolis
we plunge, enveloped by the dark expanse
and frigid air. How unlike the fiery walls

that catechism painted: shining gates
from glossy pamphlets flake rust to my touch,
and our guide, no Roman, bellows nonsense,

fumblingly seducing us lower. Still,
the crowd draws closer as stone pillars rise
to stone skies, snuffing the light. My ears pique

to moans of men whose bedroom candles burn
all night and women whose wet pillows hide
long knives to tear phantom terrors. In gloam

of green exits, I spy one woman; none
to see, my fingers brush the plaid skirt I
envision ripping. She turns, and knows, but

says nothing while I hide behind a cough.
Marching on, I bury my nose downward—
rebuked to ponder my own gut, alert

in its blindness, an appetite grown screaming
in the dark. Deeper still, hollow huts gape,
the homes six centuries forgot, the schemes

of avarice that none could know would be
someday buried beneath the glass and steel
fortresses above—a city waiting

on its own black death. Tasting twice that air
and aether, no souls rage but in my mind—
and that, perhaps, suffices. No shades breathe

their heresies and solstices in bends
and corners—still I hear them—and I muse
if others hear them too—the papist plots

and cruel apostates who once bled these walls.
We stop, informed where we now stand was once
a putrid slough, where criminals discharged

their final rites, mingling their guise with all
the trickling filth outside the gates, their end
a fitting dénouement. But not the end.

I halt, gasping for something clean. I fear
this ditch is where we'll stay, distinguishing
the screams in shadows, hearing tourist tales

of rape and murder, making out the faint,
revolting shape of bat's wings. Do I sleep?
If not, imagination conjures sin

the hand will rarely stomach; some relief
but little drink. Some stranger asks if I'm
alright but pleads me not to sit—small hope.

I nod, treacherous, damned to wander these
thick streets in coming nightmares, fleeing caves
of ice and vainly stretching for the stars.

The Wall (III.)

We wet the towel, we scrub his feet, cleanse the dirt and
    broken skin—my sister's son,
    trampled by the interloper's hooves.

Tonight we hand him to the river god, lade with gold and fire.
    We hear tense quivers in his frozen hands,
    his scream for spear and lash against invaders.

But can we, so few, assail that high road, that endless trench
    of will and magic? Free as clouds,
    are we, I tell my men, unchained by piled rocks

and the dead hand of scribbled scrolls.
    But, dare we sleep,
    our kin and Tuatha's generations strike us cowards—

and no debt will the spirits honor. We sit around the fire—
    many pitched in pitch—while my second sings,
    I mourn, and scheme the dawn attack.

I'd ask the wisdom of the stars,
    but they've gone mute,
    dimmed by the false brilliance of the city miles away.

That glow has captured many of our own: they see its safety,
    lust for its markets, bread, and wares,
    prefer its filth to ours. But light is not for sale, I say,

not owned by armored men with wicked gods.
    So at morn we'll fight,
    and I make fast my soul to meet my sister's son.

Rabbinic Pastorals

The Shepherd's Promise

What good will?
Where waits this better age?

We imagined flocks
under a clear night sky,
not soundbites or reels
of data or antipodal conquests.

Men house themselves in inky pulp
and yesterday's sensation on concrete cots.
The stench of decay mixes with bleach
and other lies in the palaces of kings.
Blood measureless by gallons pours
from plows and pitchforks
as stumps rot open in the dust.

What good will?
What works on earth?

The evening answers thus:
you now can see them,
know their worth,
and sing of peace to all.

The Shepherd's Coming

No peace but in the deep—
    the grave of unknowing.
No rest but after battle,
    lost or won but done.
No joy but in the deaf
    and frightful waiting.
No sigh until the rise
    from water's death.

And only then,
from our knees,
will we feel the flowing air
and touch the running wave
and quiet earth
and grasp the bursting stars
and together know the mercy.

Round Table Rivals

The lion sings his sinews,
cords rising and falling like red tide,
his mane electric, a chain
ready to hurl anchor.
His jaw bends, the sunlight of blood
dancing madly on the tongue.
He swallows, hungering for death,
and with God and ten thousand grandfathers
leaps.

The unicorn buries her tip deeper
into the leaves, snipping with rolling eyes
away from riper fruit dangling at the hem.
She wanders the glade, dressing herself
with light and breeze until inevitable
discovery, passionate for life.
Her ears shift with danger at the soft
feet's padding, whispering she must
fly.

*

The sage paints pictures
from his cloister window, muses
upon this perpetual chase,
contemplates desires he might touch—
power, instinct, lust. Or,
could I find higher yearnings, he
wonders, scribes out a line,
and for glory, eternity, choice, he
plucks.

Near this spot stood the house in which Sir Walter Scott was born, 15th August 1771

She reads the sign again.
                    The road resumes,
Two hundred ninety-eight windows, four ours,
Glaze down on Guthrie Street, not lifeless glass
Nor welcome tapestries—blurred mirrors, blank
To widen artist's vistas and excite
The paranoiac's nerves. And how long did
These witnesses awake to count the bairns
Delivered in its floors and flats: stillborn
Or christened, reared and grown, eventually
Forgotten by the living in churchyards—
Or, if unlucky, by the chastening
Of history.
                    But posterity burns
Without a marker, she intones, unlocks
The flat door, brushing up against its worn,
Greyed Georgian frame. Still, to know that here, once
Among the vernix, blood, and water flows,
A moment came, climaxed, and passed again—
And though our eyes saw not, unsharpened then,
Can now not unsee ghosts.
                    Perhaps, as in
A film it plays, effortless like her brew
Of nettle leaf: a montage races vast
Impressions for our illumination.
His mother's uninspiring labor, screams
Breeching under the shadowed cast of death,
Her hollowing out by a haloed child
In a Baroque portraiture. And in each scene

To follow, life unlocks like tumblers in
A common keyhole as the mundane boy
Becomes a carpenter.
                            Above the lane,
No gaping tower on Prince's Street, it lends
A whisper in the crowd, an artifact
To incarnate the Bride, the Knight, the gore
Of grim Culloden Moor—each his stories,
Each ours, discarded viciously, each lost
In countless, faceless lives—but resurrect
In words on a hundred yellowed pages
In a million libraries and stores. Thought—
Reflected, turned over, and remembered—
Issues a world that might not be known.
                                          Or
Might, she ponders, straining to catch a glimpse
Through the amorphous glass, her fingers laced
Around the cup, fame's flame starts rival sparks
In neighbor hearths, swelling to local tales
For parasitic strangers. Later, years
After death, in the gleaning archivist's
Wake, devotees' need for reliquaries
Burned, their tongues still thirsting to remember
Something.

Emhain Ablach

A slate horizon keeps none captive
who'd gaze with eyes eternal,
but the merciless wind on a lurid sea
snuffs bonfires into used tallows
and crushes the wan voyager.

He sits, a king in his armchair,
lit in the frozen light of spring's first dawn,
watching static waves rage listless.
Hungry, he gingerly stirs the stone tor,
seeking a white sail in the window
to light the perpetual mist,
spreading his mind in every crevice
for an undiscovered pin.
                                    And still
the feathered bed seduces him,
the cankered sword weightless on his fleece,
the ache of content vibrating
through every breath and hollow.

Her footsteps on the stairs a dial,
she strides within without a courteous knock,
her long locks reminiscent of a woman
he knew well but none too true.
She raises from among her armaments
a bowl of fried apples and a smile.

What sorrows weigh on such a morn,
she asks, and offers him a tray,
ignoring the ambivalent shrug
of his hand.

Grief cannot be your store
in such a seat, where star
and ocean dance, where dreams
awake on tapestries, where nature
tailors to a woman's touch.
You'd trade not these changeless days
for Glastonia's treacherous tarns,
nor would its icy meres forgive your faults
nor heal your hurts—
which someday soon shall heal.
Remember how we three bore you,
love and honor befit your rank,
apportioning our hospitality
in this lavish citadel.
Why bind
yourself, dear brother, with filaments
of happiness beyond?
Too broken, she, you won't recall,
too sod with sad disloyalty;
true, penitent he, yet still he harbors
in desire, would break all earthly vows
of court or priest to drink the tempest.
The world has also since moved on:
few out there peer through broken frames
and ancient books, too filled
with dread of purpose to pray
for your return.
Retire, my lord,
take your delight of ease,
for though we'd cling to glassy ocean rocks,
the withered fig of men cannot repair
the mortal wound.
Take breakfast, let us break
these daily walks on empty parapets
and hermetical debates.
Leave glory now to younger men.

who, unwise and inexperienced,
yet still must test their strength
upon the ruin of the earth.
Raise not your dread of plague
and inquisition, of bloodshed, bureaucrat
and atom; such days must come
in despite of the throne.
And if the crown still perched your brow
would not the mob resent your table?
Or does the cocked eyebrow quick forget
a hobbled commonwealth,
with its name and scepter
spread across a burning continent?
The tattered scroll of history is raped
by idealists and diabolists alike—
and so alike they whisper.
                              Come,
earth holds no wonder for the spirit.
Shall we recline and heal this grievous hurt
and let the meal work. A worried mind
shall never soothe. I'll even sheathe
that blade for you and leave it till some morrow—
the day, I'm sure, not distant far,
when you'll take up your armor and return.

The king receives her gifts, lays no response
to words worn true by use. She slips away,
he munches apples, no cup to cleanse his palate,
and every bite a phantasy
of a court, a sage, and brothers,
the picture of a girl astride a bed—
his dream his heaven's horror,
and he a rusted lyre with golden, broken strings.
Eyes weakening, he rubs his temple, tries
to spy a sail, and shuffles to his bed,
straining to hear the trumpet of the deep.

A British Thanksgiving

is not what you'd expect:
no crowded placemats,
no children nipping at your food,
no boxed ears, nor arguments at table.

lacks the pilgrim feel of yore,
but trades one conquest for another—
or maybe we criticize too harshly,
judging a generation by its supposed betters.

returns the sacred fowl
and grandma's dressed stuffing
for purple taters from the Farmer's Market
and a roast chicken from Sainsbury.

delays for want of things most needful,
aborted till we make a second walk
to Lupe Pintos for an American can
of pumpkin and a case of A&W.

goes quiet after prayer
without the worry of whose family
we must navigate this year—
a wishbone's hope half granted.

preludes Christmas out of season,
sharing a peppermint latte outside Starbucks
and watching fireworks spark the Festival,
thankful for the silence of ingratitude.

Snow at Morning

The shift in light
awakes the sooty street,

first in dawn's orange burning,
then a cold bath of white

silhouettes against a gentle
razor blue sky.

Newborn eyes crystalize
like Saul on the damascened road,

realizing truth was not what you sought
but the blank stillness

of your soul
and a fresh retreat

from the banality
of flickering candles.

A Midwinter Song

The chaste moon cackles over fields of white
and pours its pregnant wrath upon
a black crepe sky where seems the sun
will never rise
nor fill its run
on this, the longest night.

Beneath her blushing falseness tramps a lone
and lonely hireling; bit with frost
in callouses and cuts, near lost
to winter's plows,
gust swept and crossed
as ponderous limps he home.

There stands his hovel drowning in the snow,
patched keep befitting such a lord
of rented dirt, wages' reward:
each corner damp
and each cracked board
invites the wind to blow

within to rake and rage the crumbling hearth.
The solemn glow of this yule's log
burns low, a fitting epilogue
to stillborn days
and demagogues,
response of empty earth.

Where vestals mock his bed and vacant chair
and flames burn memories, he begs
an invocation for but dregs

and lees of life,
    bending his legs
  to any gods who'd hear.

Cold answers. He coughs, thumbs his violin,
    and with its strings draws silvery prayers,
    its notes ascend celestial stairs,
        or so he thinks,
        dispels his tears,
    blames neither Jove nor Odin.

Then, from the desert, a Judean breath
    spreads north from Caspia to Rus,
    westward to Macedon—a truce
        twixt Orient
        and Dover, sluiced
    cross earth to slip cruel Death.

And through his casement toward the East he spies
    aloft a newborn star, a light
    like rainbow rapiers splintering night,
        gags lunar laughs,
        and turns contrite
    the funerary skies.

From soul to snow the notes arise: he sings
    an unknown tune when how now full
    and decked in buds unseasonal
        the Virgin maid
        removes her shawl
    to greet the good Czech king.

He hymns of how the dissipated thief
    and outcast harlot brook the streams
    of grace: once scorned, now sympathy

they share with saints
around a tree
to find elusive peace.

He hums a wordless line, a lingering key:
for if the heavens dance anew,
might not time turn and hope subdue
the sterile grave's
stone certitude,
crescendo toward one Day?

The smiling solitary plays in awe
his infant song, the child's refrain
in aging hands made new again
in dawn's crisp air
resounds. And then
the ice begins its thaw.

Keeping Feast

Life is lived in ordinary time:
reaching for ripe avocados,
building columns from numbers
late in office millstones,
dividing lights from colors,
and washing stained utensils
to the scratched vinyl of children's tunes
in an illusory marathon of beachfront living.
In the laughter of table conversation
and the topographic cocktail flutter,
in the throbbing question at the red light
and the fear of the green,
in the desperate desert heat,
we wander.

Life is loved in sacred time
when light dances from last year's tapers
and shepherds drink wine with kings.
In the poetry of pulpit and pallet,
when the stone drinks rain
and comes to know its hollow in the brook,
the hymn and road cycle home.
When the belly shouts its voluntary grumbles,
the mind returns to a dusting of snow
and the burst of cherry blossoms.
The seasons turn familiar
and the old renews again
in the time here
and the time not yet to come.
In the echoes of oasis,
we hope.

If life is lived in time
but loved in sometime else,
when then will time
bring love to life?

The Meadows

At first, he walks beside,
his golden paw fit tight in mine,
craning up to see through eyes
that understand angelic heights
he cannot reach, while I'm inclined
  to quake with doubt.

But then, he aches to force
a separate walk—no hands, of course—
before breaking for the slope,
and I squeeze wisdom from this stone
in vain before he stands alone
  to race the steppes.

And now, a quiet gait,
filling the silence that I then craved
with guilty calls to set my pace
with his, those tall legs smooth and glazed
bronze with youth, my own neck pained
  to see how he sees.

One day, when shuffling
with titanium aid, I'll pause to think
of him, and these collected sheaves;
perhaps then I'll not fear to blink
nor walk alone in fields unseen—
  each day a breath.

Upon Climbing Arthur's Seat

Past Holyrood I hike, assume a casual air,
    A vacant cross in sacred lands,
    Unwelcome flag beneath the mountain's glare—
No pilgrim's cloak I clutch nor palmer's staff I stand.
      The hurons coast a hillside pond,
        Their flight a garbled song
      For lovers, hands clasped, oracles
    Whispering above the city to un-thong
Its fickle, secret lusts, the grief historical.
      I surge with martyr's ghosts and idols' paschal limbs;
        A lone, robed woman strolls the crest
        Aloft, a picture of antiquity or hymn
          From some schismatic kirk
          Or pagan grove. I muse,
            Almost, if she's passed or true—
          Yet is not the past still true?
        One ruined church wall her defense,
        One page in history her dance
        And every space a queue.
          So here the earthworn steps I climb,
          My escort mute savant of time.

Nothing so peaceful as a field, static in red,
    Rolling swells, metamorphic stills
  Of liquid grain, a mystic table spread
For thirsting earth and desperate faces. Yet the chills
    Of spring winds cut my body when
      I dare look up to ken
    The fiery mount. So far away
  In lecture halls I'd see primeval hills

But never dreamed to follow. Here I stand midst gray
    And murky skies, must turn back or recount the time
      By crossing bridges yet unseen.
   Rising, I glimpse the Parliament and Castle, ride
      A sea of stone above
      The dense metropolis.
        Scott's cairn, an ebenezer sits
        Of Pan's premature death knells.
    My mind, seized by the Druid's spell,
   Dredges the Forth, pulls ships from brine
    And salt below. Like these hells,
      I wonder, will this sacred stone
      Still stand, remain a holy throne?

Mounting the jagged, uncut stair, without my eyes
    I spy a mystic Island far.
  Seen from below, these hills seemed smooth, disguised
Grass diadems, but here I watch the battling stars—
    The rough ground turned to weathered slag
      Turned again to sharp spikes, ghost flags
   Of beast and crown and blade. No sign
  Nor artifact remains—save idle sloth
Of crumbling concrete calling wanderers to a line.
      Here behold the seat of crack and crevice where
      The dragon bursts beneath and melts
      The earth with savage breath—a tale sufficient heir
       To truth. What deeds of Celts
       And Romans in this waste
        Were waged? Did Galahad the chaste
        Fill the perilous siege? Gawain slay
      His giant? Lancelot gaze slant
     In tilt? Did David wrest his lance
    From these volcanic rocks? Today,
       Shall we rise and recall Logres?
       Upon the heights such questions rest—

For better not to fashion heaven's rust
In the yet untaught of earthly dust.

High Street Bazaar

Here on High Street, where St. Giles
and St. David hold palaver
in stony silence,

where the painted lady sells her wares
and street performers dance on
hands, inverted limbs and lives,

where the hill crests high enough to catch
the salt sea air, and a sliver of blue firth
can be spotted down the road,

where, the other way, the walkers
and beaters trudge up the slope
where castle wars with sky,

where the smell of whisky and the digital sounds
of pipes cascade from every
tourist shop and pub—

the pipes, those endless, horrid, beautiful beasts
that bridle the barbarous Scottish wind
and burst with rough delight,

and I, a stranger to their stories, long to merge
mine with theirs, still push against the tunes
and a history not meant for me—

here, the chaos of the streets, no Araby
nor Cheapside, still brings an awful,
loud repose to whet the soul

or sheathe in solace.

Holiday in Amsterdam

Scratch several buckets off the list at once:
an early breakfast with Anne Frank and lunch

at Café Voor Hard Rock, some novelty,
then on to Van Gogh's house for pics and tea;

see Centraal Station, as my son asks why
history filched his favorite Disney ride;

turn down the wrong street, wander through red lights
and smoke, my son oblivious, my wife

shocked tastefully; move east, still west, and see
the gangly rowhouses, thin realty

adorned with pastels and bolds hanging on
their Martian skeletons; pass over long

Venetian waterways and wander through
Glaswegian markets scavenging for blue

Vermeers; bivouac on a short boatel,
make awkward love on a twin where the bells

of St. Nicolaas ring, the city's prize;
reproduce and reproducing, we size

and laud the Philadelphian architects
like glazing liberty in Soviet

chateaux; and holiday in Europe's most
American repose, a gold signpost

toward other signs—which, somehow we forgot
to read by birth or creed or will. We ought

know vows of rings and treaties have a life
short-lived but hoped we'd somehow brook the strife

through planned avoidance; yet these short escapes
stall problems couples and all nations face,

with something gained, of course,
suspecting something lost in the divorce.

Stag Night

Waking stiff,
    transverse a gorgeous nurse,
        a Scottish mouth in fresh-pressed scrubs,
        staring past the racing shrubs,
    ambivalent to my verse.

Strange visions
    pulse with harsh percussions
        in my head, as last evening whence
        Glenfiddich followed Guinness—
    some sozzled London motions—

and some bird,
    not too unlike this nurse, dressed
        for her birthday while my mates
        sang double-handed tunes. A break
    in my memoir at the depot. Pressed,

the train slows
    past gardens, screams its oboe,
        the call of the conductor sings
        we've reached Edinburgh—but I think
    I've an appointment home in Soho—

the happiest,
    doubtless, of my life. For then
        at noon, my lady—not this nurse—
        stands at altar; and I'll vow her
    not to repeat these nights again.

But it's now
    seven early; this jolly prank
        will end with a furious trouble
        and strife, fees non-refundable
    and purgatory in the banque.

Open doors
    close my eyes. Should I change this hearse?
        turn home to face their jeers,
        her wrath—or dare career
    my chances with the Scottish nurse?

Two Bodies

Prince John's Subjects

> *Agricola et vitam et fortunam nautae saepe laudat;*
> *nauta magnam fortunam et vitam poetae saepe laudat;*
> *et poeta vitam et agros agricolae laudat.*
>
> —Horace, Sermones

The Farmer to His Crops:

> If only I'd been born a lord
> With fields and men at my command.
> But God saw fit to craft these hands
> To labor in the rising sun,
> This soil a pen, my plow a sword,
> Tomorrow's future now begun.

The Lord to His Scribe:

> If only I'd been born a son
> Second to my noble house,
> Divided Fortune turn me mouse.
> Yet these hands fit to pray
> Serve God with coin, his wise will won,
> Divine hours marking out the day.

The Friar to His Bed:

> If only I'd been born to spray
> And seed and fertilize the land,
> Await green yield from hills of sand,
> My potentates my gourds.

But still I'll serve hands laced each day,
My cell a field, my waist of cords.

Prince Charles' Subjects

*Our civilization is in danger of going down to
destruction in an orgy of hatred.*

—Bertrand Russell, The Conquest of Happiness

The Clerk to Her Steno:

If only I could be a star, an Aubrey, Posh, or a Britney,
Black Ray-Bans blocking out the sun and flashes
As I pose with fans at restaurants and post
For a million followers or more
Instead of doodling erotic stick figures
During my boss's budget ramblings.

The MP to His Mirror:

If only I'd not have to bend
To every Bob and Fanny's whims
On some union vote or other.
My sore throat only chirps,
This sagging chin holds high,
Because others' voices screech.

The Musician to His Guitar:

If only I was rich enough
Or found my long-lost soul
On a beach in black Ray-Bans
Like in all the songs I sing.
But maybe life is just a dream
And our souls the stuff of worn cliches.

The Dragon

If all history could be written, caught
on wind: to see the horror rise in ire,
her awful wings enchanted, grace in flight

balletic; then, unable to avert
our gaze, her apex suddenly erupts,
the spine turns, bowels glowing with heat—she starts

a sudden descent as the margins light
with sulfuric fear, mix of breath and fire,
and all the elements dissolve in thought.

An Unextraordinary Death
Recorded Nov. 18, 1799

The proxy penitent—
condemned, he feels the hands
push forward like so many spoons
and knives mangling their luncheon
in civilized rebuke.

The mobbed Grassmarket
rots and jeers his family name
and roars the demster's dark pronouncement—
one final ride down Old Nick's tail
for someone else's vice.

While he ascends his oaken dais,
those grim spectators here
for more than holiday peek through
reputed blindfolds, statuesque
in the spreading terror's face.

But comes unexpectedly
a kindly, firm embrace of dark-eyed hood
and somber noose. Arched brows
arise among the stilted shouts,
a hot noon tea in snow-swept winter tones.

A joyous antic of his own indignity,
kneeling between crown and cross,
standing before horde and charter,
a splash of blood stains the mind,
and the lift of the blade stretches the universe.

*Scattered Pages from the New College Library
on the Mound*

Immortal wreathed in clover—
Enigma for the heart

An acorn in the palm—
Contentment in the cosmos

Mercy in a crumb—
The essence in an act

A breath upon the waters—
In every thought and motion

Light within the sound—
All matter wrapped in a parabola

Argyll and Bute

Argyll and Bute is one
    of thirty-two unitary
authority council areas
    and a lieutenancy area
        (pronounced left-tenant-see).

      The administrative center is Lochgilphead
        (no English pronunciation possible).
            West of Loch Lomond,
            North of the Firth of Clyde,
            and East of Loch Long.

The main railway line
    is the West Highland Line,
        which links Oban to Glasgow.

    Due to its heavily
        indented
    coastline and many islands,
ferries are in wide use,
    as part of the council transport system,
the main ferry being Caledonian MacBryne.

Part of *From Russia with Love* (1963)
    was filmed here,
      and, of course,
Paul McCartney sang of us
    in "Mull of Kintyre."

But no guidebook, broken in cascades of words,
prepares you for the eloquence
of caressing, warring elements
where water blends with hill,
and as you plunge into the mirrored lochs,
the fingers of another earth
enfold you with her touch,
and you suddenly know
you knew neither the world
nor yourself.

Standing Stones

What, then, I wonder, are these standing stones,
  a lazed half mile from some hinter B road,
    a cloister ringed by hushed Gregorian hills?
Why here no brown signs, no historic ode
  to pipe us to the spot, no past distilled
    to textbooks by a trousered bureaucrat?
Just a chance plunge through the pass and the shrill
  command of my toddler bids me turn back
    in time—small marvel, thus, so few should greet
this scene since Tacitus. We traipse and track,
  no Caledonians we, our heavy feet
    in search of rubbish from a furtive tryst
or cultic reverie, but no such seat
  is seen—just trees and frozen heather kissed
    by Boreas and these dark, faceless masks.
Were these to chart the moons, these monoliths,
  enmark the turns of history, their tasks
    to mark or murder time? Could these be graves
remarking the undead? What hallowed casks
  of myth remain, engraved by waves
    by some sea god who once to graves sent men
with grave expression? Were these heartsick staves
  from prince to peasant girl whose lord again
    refused to share his heritage? Or why,
if just memorials of Cuchulainn's son
  descending like a Kaaba in the sky,
    did Aphrodite rise up from the spray—
angelic fancy or a battle cry?
  To the red Audis racing past each day
    a monument stands an apathetic gong,

while the pilgrim lifts one shell castaway
and finds a shore of relics. Before long
    we bare the naked, discomfit truth: thrones
are never raised for centuries, nor songs
    composed for generations come. Alone,
    the architect builds not for us but for
himself. And as he crafts, we skip our stones.

The Wandering Lass

There's a lass I see oft
    As I pass through the highlands,
    A lass I know well in my dreams;
And the lass that I know
    Strays far from the road,
    Calling life is not all that it seems.

She rides a bay stallion
    As the wind bites her dress,
    Alone but with hope unafraid,
In search of a lover
    Estranged but not gone
    With whom she had once spent her days.

By day the gray heavens,
    By night the home fires,
    As ever she sings out his name;
And her voice races rocks
    And the hills and the moors,
    Crying empty returns of the same.

So many boys stolen
    By thresh, press, or mine,
    Or by fairies that lure lads away.
But she'll cross wild hills,
    Howling moors and the rocks
    To take them both home on her bay.

There's a lass I see oft
  As I pass through the highlands,
  A lass I know well from my dreams;
And the lass that I know
  Strays far from the road,
  Calling love is not all that it seems.

Monastic in Absentia

Beyond the cloister, there I found
    A vision once bereft me
In the fences of the order,
    My water turned to wining.

We parted praying hands and fast
    Our bodies like as worship,
And drunk with love's divining froth
    We wed in earthen purchase.

Now, at her altar genuflect,
    Prostrate in our bed for years;
Murmuring a liturgy, I
    Meditate and find my fear.

My gift a cup to love Him more,
    Or idle draft to sleep?
Love others—children, kin, and king?
    What rule do I dare keep?

To serve the poor would honor God;
    To serve my wife might more.
Lapsed postulant, can I bend all
    Through one kenotic door?

The Chapel

A mark on the map wants a legend yet
    Demands a name. A steeple rises high
Before the mountain range on the town's edge,
    Vestige from a former mass. Fructified
    With good, and wet with moss, the spirit's work
Spread far from the cathedral, consecrate
    By callused hands. For in this modest kirk,
    The flock worked twelve score years to pray and break
    The essence, bury souls in water, rise
In grave, and rest their frames within the yard
    And sight of heaven's storehouse. Few despised
    Their common lot, and all were keen to guard
      Their parish tales, awaiting common doom
      And mourners chanting letters on a tomb.

But bellows, belts, and smoke arrest the wheels
    Of seasoned time, and many tenants won
With promises of cropless wealth appealed
    Their gods of stomach, pride, and kingdom. None
    Asked after water, nor about the souls
Laid in the yard. Their body languishing,
    The church sold to a troupe, who cast the rolls
    To refuse, screened the altar, turned crossing
    To a stage. Each night, stories breathed to life
By Shakespeare, Shaw, and locals there amassed,
    Replayed the ritual of mortal strife,
    Recovered some communion in a mass
      Of human questions and angelic truth—
      A shade of whimsy claimed the parish youth.

With breath of earth exhausted, thus the stacks
　　Of brick and bones reached sadly in the scape,
And those who left its skeletons and jacks
　　Refused to mount the stage, distracted shapes
　　In the radiated glow of dancing screens.
Its coffers bare, the troupe could not perform
　　On rotting planks with drapes unravelling;
　　What wood remained was reinforced, transformed
　　To tables fit for food while diners spoke
Hushed tones above their plates and overlooked
　　The mountain range by candlelight, awoke
　　A revelation without word. But brooked
　　　　By patrons questioning the churchyard rows,
　　　　The owner laughed and pled he did not know.

Highland Dreams

Sometimes I wake at night with the smell
of iced pine, a phantom mist surrounding
and I remember each breath a cold fire
washing the lungs like breaking glass. I blink
through images of wild trees piercing
the white blanket, dancing priests shouting
their prayers against an unforgiving, heretic wind.

Ever a portal through the glass of time
in worlds unchanging and changeable.
I hear the dawn march of Urquhart
and tremble underneath the alien Storr shadow.
Each step presses down in the muddy layers
of seven civilizations, rises with the strength
of seventy thousand spectres.

So many spectres in the burning fog:
king, warrior, prince, and poet—claimants
refusing to lose themselves in Lethe,
boasting the unicorn freedom
of riotous self-rule, long preceding
Arborath, protectants of the prophetic voice
trumpeted by these hills.

A creek passes cleft where water, winter's
fugitive defeat, rides beside a bed of yellow violet.
I warm with the vision, rinse my hands
in the stabbing cold, and settle in
with a familiar voice on the wind
turning mountains into roads
and raising up all my highways.

Midday, I ponder to what savage depths
the Ness plunges, reaching down into
the very core of things, and to what heights
the Glencoe cliffs thrust, rising over
its Pictish descendants but bowing
before the hand that made them. To walk
these lands is to ask the cosmic question.

Pressing on, I see the clash of baskethilts
and tartan, feel the horse under my legs
and a bonnie lass gripping hard behind me.
We dance the ceilidh in the village, take in
its rhythm, an imprint on our souls. Finding a cabin
beneath a summer downpour, we escape the banks
and omnibuses of tomorrow's tyranny.

In that magic, the sun warms the cool skin
of an autumn breeze, freezing the throat
and numbing the limbs. I reach down
into the rich soil, look up at the exploding stars
still fixed by northern charts
and catch in my periphery the gold
and crimson dance of the trees.

And ever do clouds like rolling waterfalls
descend, upend, and spend themselves
upon the rocks, flowing around each mountain
like heaven's walls girding earth's
adamantine towers. Should they crumble
one day, these are the hills I'd ask to fall
and cover me, ruinous against an obsidian sky.

Her breath beside me falls, fills again.
A frost leaves her lips, and though I'd ask
if she shares my dreams, I snuggle under a quilt
of nostalgia—whispers of inertia—

bury myself in a pillow of fear and close
my eyes to the harmonies
of chanting pipes like the land's beating heart.

Waystations

I.

Accused, the bitter home I flee,
    Of love's presumed betrayal slip the sting.
    At St. Austell's railway the wheels turn
As moon mountains glow stark
    And bitter under stars
Where no confessor soothes the burn—
    The Lyonessean tree.

II.

Heavy lies the weight of Euclid's lines,
    And heavier the strain of Plato's scribe,
    Still heaviest the tendons of the heart.
Reliving to transgress,
    My slipping thoughts arrest
Past Plymouth: another rock apart,
    An anchor or a spline.

III.

At Bristol Station I alight,
    Glance back toward where the River Avon sighs
    And thence where bathes the ancient citadel.
My mind grasps cottage stones,
    No penance may atone;
To linger brings no north, no bells
    Jubilant, no candle light.

IV.

She sits across, a linen sign
    Of favor. Though her newspaper divides
    Us, still a Cardiff poise surrounds her face.
Her hair a rich Merlot,
    Her smile deep, merciful,
And must, I muse, rise for my place—
    My doubts dissolve in wine.

V.

A stranger stands beside, makes claim
    Somewhere near Liverpool, lends voice and leans
    A shoulder close to share his mundane work.
The countryside slips past,
    His tenor smooths the path
With lullabies of village kirks
    To bear my woolen shame.

VI.

The gliding lakes, a holy place,
    And vision of a lady stooped to bless.
    She gazes at my tears, holds each drop like
A child collects the sea,
    Dries lilac from my lees,
Our mutual gratitude a spike
    On winding tracks of grace.

VII.

Staid, thrust on the route from Carlisle,
    A castle of beautiful chimeras,
    The kiss of Judas conjures wistful touch,

And like the king I quake
        And dread the drunken ache,
Lest I list in amnesic clutch
        Toward Alba many miles.

VIII.

The lowlands ring the capital,
        The lurching train descends. I hear the small,
        Hunched nuns who entered at the last stop cry;
Priest dead or abbey burned,
        They mourn the past and yearn
For stronger oaks. I sympathize
        In hopeful whispers dull

IX.

Yet stumble on the Stirling cross.
        I reach to wrench the brake, abort the coarse
        Retreat and salve my shuddering sinews; yet
A tower climbs the crest
        Far off, an echoed rest
Of where I tend. The ghost bridge whets
        Resolve and fires the dross.

X.

All pages stripped at Inverness,
        I disembark, take in this final fess,
        Last cursed light of a people I still love.
I mount a coach and glance
        The snow draped peaks—what dance
Might lilt in highland vaults above?—
        But press on nonetheless.

XI.

Some wandering road past rocky shoals
    As dawn approaches; yet my body—cold,
    Fixed, and raised in place—suffocates with weight
Of passive action. I
        Ken not these hills and sigh,
For, know, the conscience of the night
        Disturbs the guilty soul.

XII.

The world ends in Thurso Norse,
    A pleasant thought. No lorry nor no train
    May draw beyond the sand. No need to take
In Celtic art nor see
        St. Pete's. No memory
But salt air. Thus, I contemplate
        Oblivion up north.

XIII.

And yet I find the ferry crew,
    My shivering arms unshaken by the jolts
    Of wind. In blinding light I grope the dark;
My Lot, I think, his islands
        In the reach, what wild strands
Lured you to abandon me? Or
        Did I abandon you?

XIV.

That hoary king once ruled this cope,
    Someone else's realm, someone else's globe;
    And I might sail by someone else's goad.

But will it be Orkney
     Or further on Norway
Or Valhalla? I know no road,
     I cannot say but hope.

The Ballad of Rory Munro

Good Rory worked his family farm,
    By ken and wit reared sheep by day;
By candle used his strong left arm
    To paint his landscapes lite and gray.

In village round he'd share his oils:
    For miles they marveled at his light
And shadow, claiming talents spoiled
    On witless sheep would be benight'd.

A neighboring laborer did brand
    Him stealing sheep, unlucky feints;
Though Rory pled his guiltless hands,
    The village turned and burned his paints.

Then Rory's kin in Moray Firth
    Drowned deep beneath the blackened waves,
And Rory stumbled on the earth
    To stand as head of clan and clay.

The clans condemned his lawless theft,
    An envious eye t'would lust and roam,
Yet Rory shrugged for what was left,
    And said he just defend't his home.

Their neighbor feud—Clan Ross—resumed
    Their marches' raids with Rory's rise.
No more, the Munro's council said,
    We must strike now and Ross surprise.

The men are armed, the plan's prepared;
    The first Munro before ye 'pproved.
We dare not wait for Ross to bear
    His teeth. Good Rory did approve.

He marched the Clan in swift attack
    And slit their villain unawares.
Munros lift'd him upon their backs;
    Ross called him tyrant bending theirs.

At this, Clan Murray offered forth
    White flags and tribute to this laird,
While large Clan Sutherland up north
    Drove south for war with gun and sword.

The clans condemned his lawless theft,
    An envious eye t'would lust and roam,
Yet Rory shrugged for what was left,
    And said he just defend't his home.

Too armed for peace, Clan Sutherland
    Had warned, too close to sign a pact;
Before Munro might swipe their land
    Must they the blackguard strike and sack.

So Rory split his men, charged troops
    Out west around Loch Shin, shipped fleets
Out east along the coast, made loops
    And did his enemy unseat.

Upon the victory he made
    A merry gathering, and all
Pledged fealty, plus Clan Mackay,
    Mackenzie, Fraser in the hall.

No treaty e'er would Clan Macleod
　　Accept, but cursed him under ban;
When Rory's kin shunned more war clouds,
　　He cried, "Dread God, and fear no man."

The clans condemned his lawless theft,
　　An envious eye t'would lust and roam,
Yet Rory shrugged for what was left,
　　And said he just defend't his home.

He sued for peace, but Clan Macleod
　　With Lewis and of Harris bond'd
Their families as one, a proud,
　　Great Clan defending Scotland's sons.

Nor would they wait, allow some thief
　　To swallow farm and level hill,
Who drowned his kin to rise as chief,
　　For shipwrecks paid the witch's bill.

The Clans Sinclair and Gunn dared not
　　Oppose Good Rory's waxing force,
And swore defense against the lot
　　Macleod had cast in his war course.

The clans marched out, their armies met
　　At Ulapul upon the braes;
For three long days they made their threats,
　　For three long days they spit and brayed.

The clans condemned his lawless theft,
　　An envious eye t'would lust and roam,
Yet Rory shrugged for what was left,
　　And said he just defend't his home.

Some say that Rory's sure foot slipped,
    While others swear he was betrayed,
A few believed he lost his grip;
    But he was broomed upon the braes.

On moothill, brieve and council met
    To try Good Rory's lawless deeds:
Accused of warring, racking debt,
    Kinslaying, and vile sorcery.

But Rory, tame, made no defense,
    Resigned to face the prison halls;
He kindly asked for oils and thence
    Did paint his landscapes on his walls.

Years later, aft Culloden Moor,
    The British tore the prison 'part,
Found Rory's cell, his walls and floors,
    Looked o'er and loudly mocked his art.

The clans condemned his lawless theft,
    An envious eye t'would lust and roam,
Yet Rory shrugged for what was left,
    And said he just defend't his home.

Voices of Iona

The deck sways, the mainland lost behind,
skies so blue striking violet,
their dark white clouds
winding upward to gently crush
this erratic palmer. My breath
catches, a fish on line, when the pilot
points obviously down the street to the abbey,
and all around the bare rock
scraped like an Easter tonsure,
this last isle a holdfast
against the wine dark deep.
But I turn to the village, past tartan
and whisky shops where martyrs sleep
and kings lie loudly, their graves
raised glasses, toasts to names
not wholly forgotten but unknown.
One keep, a middling man of the yew,
pours me a drink in tones of the cloth.

Did you know, he asks,
        with the loyal timbre of generations of barmen,
that the good doc Johnson
once called this soil fruitful ground?
        Fruitful?
        Aye, but poor. Take care,
        he warns,
the Island don't taint your heart with too great piety.
        Thin draws the line between grief and grace.
        Here, where barbarian monks minced these sands,

and druids mingled with the saints,
    Here, where shadows draw for the world's soul,
    Here lies the dry stone
that drinks clean the waves of history,
      quakes skeptics into priests,
        and raises cowards into men—

Men like my da, a mainland hosteler,
His livelihood soda and warbled keys
Of tourists seeking same as all. One day
He shuttered up and crossed the narrow sea,
Discovering what angels caroled tunes
Along the waters. Cresting utterances
And growing sighs had drifted landward long
Years past; to learn these strange occurrences
Might satisfy his mind and dress the wound
He lacked the heart to name. So when he found
The congregation round the Great MacLeod,
Who called all wayward children to the Sound,
He understood the stirring in his blood,
Remained to dilate prayerful clamors, bread crumbs
To wrest ruins from crags and raise a throne
In its cradle, pass on the ancient thrums

Of warriors like William, a hero used
To toasting kings o'er waters, sore abused
By king's prerogative, then disavowed
The young Pretender when the turbid crowd
Had at Culloden cast out his sole son—
A cruel lesson that politics save none
Who hold them dear. Unmoored, he took to ford
The Firth and Loch and Isle with neither sword
Nor pen but pilgrim's cloak and tack to find
The fraying hem of union, to unbind

The prisoner in his soul. There, they claim,
No sacrament or rite did he exclaim,
All crosses smashed long past, he brushed the ghost
Of his son, held communion on the coast
With long discarded shades. In broken light
Of rotting chancels, thus, he spoke with Ross
Of Butte, John Campbell too, took up a gloss
With the whole MacRory line, who then led

to even he, Ranald of Somerled,
bit under bridal to rule Christ's church, fools
refusing righteous yokes and kicking goads.
So too the ancient Hebrew seed, he moans.
To plant and pray and weed and hold one's tongue
'tis no little hardship, true, but dare they
refuse the office blessed above, resist
the anchorite who wars with spirits, shun
the knees that break beneath the holy weight
of their undying souls? These barren rocks
be better soil for fruits of purer prayers.
But would a Christ find faith in this black rock?
His chest afire, he flees compline and seeps
the sands of Martyr's Bay, wails his lament.
And, buckling under the temple of stars,
red eyes from an onyx sky pry his soul
apart. The Mercy strikes him cruel and lifts
his stiffened shoulders, holds erect his soft
and trembling chin. A contemplative grin
awash, he studies his new tutor dear
to teach his budding brothers true, thenceforth
reminding them in prayer the sacred name
of Benedict, and of that blessed year

when Fenrir Guthrum surrendered knee at blessed Finian's stone—
Finian, not Columba's teacher but of his name,
that true abbot who unearthed Fenrir's soul
with his flaming eyes. Standing in the bloody foam,
Finian's hands raised like seraphs, asked life enough
to pardon the souls of every Viking
then raping the abbey and stealing
the lives of his brothers. Fenrir stayed
his blade and heard the madman's poetry,
asked what god would read the lips of godless men,
what deity would bleed to capture wayward ships,
what spirit wield pity as his spear?
And Fenrir caught that music's strain
mirrored in the beating waves
and sheathed his sword forever. He pledged
to serve the All of all men,
crowned after his war on the world tree,
swore perpetual pilgrim to the island—
and here he follows still Finian's echo,
the abbot, who, but eight years earlier,

spied the langskips on that Christmas night,
breathed dreadful prayers before the torch
lighting the faces of thirsty demons.
For twenty years he kept the shrines of Saint Columba,
shielded the renowned book,
planted the apostolic creeds,
and guided the sights of monks heavenward.
But now the end would come,
as Saint John himself revealed, prophesying fire.
At morrow's dawn the land would black to ash
as Lindisfarne and Caithness—all lamps
once lit against the nothing
swallowing up the world.
Rebuking his despair, he mouthed thanks,

resolved to storm the beach at daybreak,
and utter the final eloquence of the staff,
much as his teacher Adomnan would have done.
Oh, such a man was he,

he whose poetry was inked in stars
and chiseled into shore stones,
crafting worlds with the wood of words,
like those he carved lamenting Bridei mac Bili—
Passed into heaven's throne room is Bridei,
Third of his name, first of his virtue.
No charnel house might keep him,
No ash heap be forgotten.
The lakes shall always remember,
Dun Neichtain shall always remember
How Bridei overthrew Ecgfrith,
Destroyer of churches and servant of the serpent.
He cast the Lord's enemy down
And buried his sword point in the earth
To the cheers of the people.
Long and prosperous was his kingdom.
But to greater praise his soul rises
To bow before his High King
And inscribe his name in the Book.
Many were the tears that flowed
and longer grew the memories of Bridei
for the inscriptions passed down,
from the zealous saint Adomnan

apostle to apostles,   bewitching the green man
from the ancient trees,   touching spirits in gnarled wood
but with clenched fists   around the chalice;
such a man to weep   with each scream of innocents
on every inland breeze,   tormented in his holy soul

to raise his pen   and fatal parchment.
No longer kings be law,   nor unsheathed sword
remain unreckoned.   He scribed, repeated cries
in dale and synod   to guard the orphan,
a new Justinian   to enclose the lonely isles,
to Columbkille's land,   bring his peace:

a divine rock unearthed by man—
the Abrahamic mount.
For like the exile from Terah
so too was he in Culdreimhe's wake,
no pacifist himself.
But on this sacred edge of earth,
one bark away from paradise,
here wood and stone and souls
might mix as one,
ascend that violet sky,
and lift Saint Martin's cross.
A home for penitents and beggars
both he'd raise, that none
feel prodigal again.
And one day, as he laid
a waste-high stone and gazed
at waves unending,
touching azure bliss,
he heard the waters sing
blood's music, wondered faintly,
how Martin might have claimed this land,
and what might have Merlin done?

Everything

Everything is all we want:
to read the map of all truth
and to know all knowing

so that every piece locks
and threads together like a Gobelin tapestry.
But no ocean may be, somebody says,

swallowed in one relentless gulp,
so you narrow and shrink
and aim, choose one anything,

something you can break open and pour out
and drink deeply until it swells
your belly and scorches your lungs,

changes the depth of your eyes
and the color of your soul,
so that nothing seems same anymore—

and that anything you chose to know
becomes some eternal sea,
one thing you can only wade in

and splash upon the shore.
And later, maybe years, you lean
into your evening chair with a thick book

and ponder how you drank the cup
and beheld the ocean, how the one thing
fits together with

everything.

Leeward

But some of us came from the west,
the Dea Men from Tara. We bore regret

like spears of blood and water, guarded
a land of jade wealth, a fourth garden,

where young maids with bands of gold balanced
wine into a shattered, unbroken chalice.

So sublime our Feast of Age
that even the Gael broke through waves

to land on white shores filled
with acorns, honey, milk and fish.

So celestial our realm of emerald pearl
that we bled on the strand with the king of the world—

but none could sleep the sadness
clawing at our hearts,
nor raise our dead,
nor silence the battle din each season.

Here in the trim wastes of Iona,
the draught still fevers the head
and fingers grasp in lust. Yet here
steal only phantoms, and their raths restrain
our rage to list other whispers
and seek some signs

to hold and taste, inhale. To wait.
And in the raw defense,
this gate, we trow, houses another king
beyond the castle of sense.

Harvest Poem

The father lays his blade upon the earth,
  Soil thawed and fallow, ready to receive
His firm, unyielding prow. He parts the seas,
  A captain commandeering waves of dirt
  And wakes of fecund trails. His element
He shapes, his craft he knows from countless years
  In field. He drives, anticipating tears
  Of joy while knowing grief may come; he bends
  The rich, reluctant land to patient wrath,
Long months before designed his plan, removed
  The stones, slayed weeds, and churned with pick in truth;
  He digs his furrows for the sower's path.
    But this day, resting now he contemplates
    The harvest for the days ahead in faith.

His son immerses himself in the soil,
  Content not merely to disperse his seed,
But deftly plants each kernel to conceive
  A greater crop. His fingers, cracked and roiled,
  Run fresh with dirt and blood. No sympathy
He seeks nor indulges a youthful angst,
  But dips his cup into the bag with pangs
  Of sorrow. Wrestling with desires to concede
  And creeping doubts which weigh his weary feet—
For will his father's plan succeed? Designs
  Untested may not prove—and still he finds
  A germ of hope his work will be complete;
    For this day, learning in his solitude
    To trust, he reaps a joyful attitude.

And she who is unseen breathes soft and goes
    About her quintessential task. She sings
A gentle tune composed of mysteries
    Unfathomed since the earth and sun first rose.
    She charts their course, observes the seasons, and
Anticipates the floods with every step
    Above the soil. The notes dance off her lips
    In harmony with all the spheric bands,
    And with her loving syllables brings each
Green, infant shoot to hear her better. Now
    She smiles affectionately in knowledge how
    These secrets will unfold, small proofs to teach
        Her that this day the ancient cycles turn
        Still fruitful and the future is secure.

The field is wide, and countless verdant stalks
    Exploding toward the heavens dance upon
The breeze in silent chorus. Time has come,
    And through its waving sheaves the family walks,
    Sun drenched, to receive the waiting ears
And gather them. Then at the house, beneath
    The sunset's light they work: extract the sheath
    That long defends, remove the clinging hairs,
    Cut out the cancerous worm, and bathe the gold,
Great, glistening corn. The ripe and fully-grown—
    Though those too weak and immature are thrown
    To mulch—are now a bounty to behold;
        For in the days to come when all's dispersed,
        Their labor's fruit will fill exalted verse.

Voyager

Waiting, in harbor,
the stiff cocoon of the bay,
listen, a man learns not one
but a hundred possible lives,
a thousand ships incarnate
breathing, heaving, dreaming, cursing—
snowflakes of a white waste.
I've seen them all, lived all:
the languishing tongue,
the pupils mad and black for light,
the desperate hour—
each rhyming in desire.

Ceaseless creaking hands find countless tasks—
sails ripped and sewn, barnacles scoured, seaweed strained,
names rechristened over peeling paint on gunwales worn by
rain and sun and brine—
ignoring the shrill chorus of wind cutting the bay,
its lecherous play a scourge
upon exhausted nerves.
Worn salts walk decks of weathering timbers
refusing rot, bearing yokes of sin and age,
each timber a tale, each scar a story—
but for every winter the masters' care
holds them firm.

When a youth, listless,
looking down from the iced ridges round,
I'd rise on a northern gale,
lust for its speed
and its sinister palms of wealth,

not counting death behind its wings.
Now leathered, rigging fraying,
I know its voice, that dirge,
frenzied singing midst the floating bergs,
whistling prophets ready to unsheathe their black swords.
Those flows skulking near the slips,
broken centuries before on ships long lost,
casually find their way here
like marked assassins turning their cards
as though we might forget their devilish game.

Even so, I must dare the waters,
these endless waters, my waters,
part seam of sky and sea and find the path
through waters, waters, waters,
and pierce the world's precipice.
The land, few understand,
no native element,
slides deep into men's souls unawares.
Mending fences is an art untrue,
and a chair beside the hearth charms sleep—
sparkling rotgut piping us to doldrums.
But on the waters, the waters,
I see unveiled the frosted beard
and wicked grin of my enemy
and so front him with my will.

In a strange tongue
I make farewells to my woman and my kin,
the insane congregation.
None can interpret babel,
nor read a language tattooed on the heart.
For I know the crack of wood,
wood of deck and wood of prow,
to launch firmer feet out toward waters, waters, waters,
to tear down the scaffold,

rip back the velvet blue
and grasp the edge of nothing,
nothing,
nothing that breaks my skull,
scrapes my soul clean from the leather,
cast wildly into the deep.

In that moment
the din of battle screams,
and I dive
perilously
into the fate
that waits
for all men,
and the one—
one word—
saved just for me.

Yet here I raise the mast,
turn the wheel towards the mouth and shout this,
this, my *credo resurgam*,
wrestle with the waves
and pull myself forward
to clutch the horizon's razor.

Departing Folkestone

No ritual in farewell
for an old world snuffing its candles,
only the shimmering of dead guardians
signing valedictions
in a smoldering wick.

Pity the couple, kisses raw and savage, wet with tears.
Pity the mother, ripping herself from the fruit of her womb.
Pity the cleric, bartering books for a rifle and grenades.

We see their shadows on the shore,
embracing the filagree of lives already lost.
The mind, a wind for scents and vapors,
catches fragments real and imagined.

Pity the soldiers, buried in trenches long grassed over.
Pity the bedchamber, the laugh of its fire cold in the hearth.
Pity the gates, hunched over, no elders to lean upon its bars.

And the children, too young
to know the soldiers, too old to see us their heirs,
dance in the heather before the row houses,
painted tin soldiers sipping bliss through grails
but blind to the wraith summoning
them, too, to the posey ring.

The young flee youth, discarding it like an unused shovel in a pack.
The young smash bottles of aged wine for new flags.

In every age, the world lifts its skirts
for the maddening grape
the god War pours into his chalice.
With dark incantation his hands divide the supplicants
and pull at the threads of Venus' tapestries
to weave a world in flames.

Their elders grasp illusions and weep to see a broken chain.
Their elders, having danced this waltz before, no longer keep
    tempo.

We learned here all peoples come
to hum the apocalyptic tune,
as if to change a thing in law
would change the thing in fact,
anticipating the ravenous fiend
who rips at the world's laces.

Pity the parliament, its rhetoric damp munitions.
Pity the burning room, its treasures forever unkept.
Pity—yes, pity—the lord watching his orders obeyed
    from a wireless.
    For pity is the voice of the living
    trying to breech the suicide of the damned.

But the future waits always a tempest,
sworn to end in death. Yet beyond finality
and the pale curtain, where change
is the flame ever burning,
waits the shade of the apple tree,
where we learn to make peace
with what should never have been.

Beyond Byzantium

When sailing through the clouds the rule of feet
Holds no more sway, no calculus by glove
Or cubit. Distance here dissolves: beneath,
The elements of earth hold firm; above,
The convex dark sings taut as Pluto beats
The sky; between them lies the cloven globe
Where separated waters form a grace,
An order glimpsed in each sunset we chase.

Our vessel rises toward celestial courts,
Sublime not manifest. Most of us, bent
And blemished, take no notice of our course
As eyes stream fantasies and lose what's lent
To us in every moment—all to thwart
Dilating clocks. Dull praise and high lament
Strike relative to a rebellious youth,
A quantum curve no closer to the truth.

And though we'd fly beyond Byzantium,
All riddles turned to rust as recompense,
We'd never cut the knot nor solve the sum.
Could we break each horizon, pierce each dense
Expanse, sense senseless forms, clutch cosmic crumbs,
And seek new stars within the eminence,
We'd know less how our faith has learned the good:
That the world hangs on a few nails and wood.